{ the light at the end of the diaper pail }

The LIGHT at the END of

V

VILLARD
NEW YORK

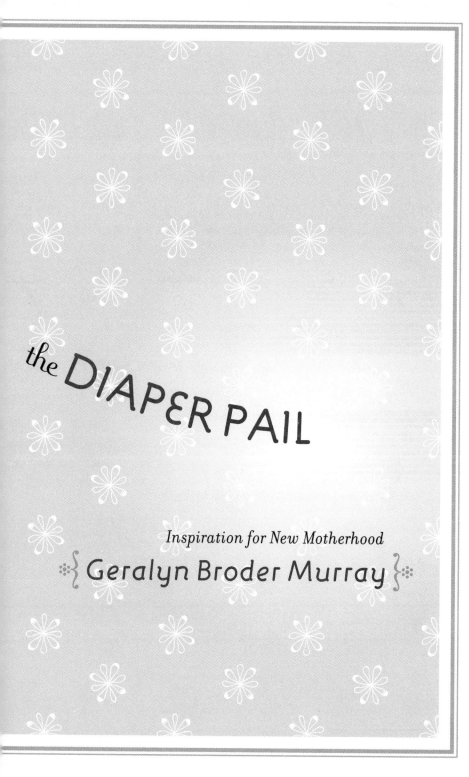

the DIAPER PAIL

Inspiration for New Motherhood

❖{ Geralyn Broder Murray }❖

Published in the United States by Villard Books, an imprint of
The Random House Publishing Group, a division of Random House, Inc.,
New York.

VILLARD and "V" CIRCLED Design are registered trademarks
of Random House, Inc.

LIBRARY OF CONGRESS CATALOGING-IN-PUBLICATION DATA

Murray, Geralyn Broder.
The light at the end of the diaper pail : inspiration for new motherhood /
Geralyn Broder Murray.
p.   cm.
ISBN 978-0-345-50585-9 (hardcover : alk. paper)
1. Mothers—Life skills guides.   I. Title
HQ759.M97 2008
646.70085'2—dc22   2007043617

Printed in the United States of America on acid-free paper

www.villard.com

9 8 7 6 5 4 3 2 1

FIRST EDITION

Book design by Simon M. Sullivan

For Reese and Finn,
my inspiration

and for Chris,
my light

introduction

My first three months of motherhood were not what I expected.

~ I suppose it was the maternal equivalent of becoming Cinderella, but in reverse: spending nine months as the belle of the ball and then, overnight, becoming an exhausted, hormonal chambermaid. And, to add insult to injury, the realization that all of the work I'd been doing preparing for labor and delivery had nothing to do with having an actual baby. What made it all the more difficult was everyone asking, "Isn't this the happiest time of your life?"

~ I wrote this for the "me" I was then. And for the millions of "mes" I know are out there, wondering when the real mother is going to show up and take care of this kid. This book doesn't need to be read straight through—unless you just can't stop yourself. Truly, my hope is that you'll be able to open to any page and get a shot in the arm: of confidence, of laughter, and mostly, of compassion.

~ Now, before you start looking for the letters and fancy titles after my name, let me just say, there aren't any. I am certainly no expert. I am simply a mom who's been there, who knows what it's like to get your world rocked by a seven-pound, two-ounce bundle of joy. To you, I say: Here is a little light to shine on your brand-new, sometimes rocky road. May this book be a friendly companion as you make your way toward becoming exactly the kind of mother you never dreamed you could be.

{ the light at the end of the diaper pail }

1

 There is a certain
attractiveness to sweats.

2

It is okay to really, really enjoy *A Baby Story* on The Learning Channel.

You do not have to tell any of your non-baby friends this.

3

 You have permission to
pretend you don't hear stupid questions like,

"How is he sleeping?"

4

Chocolate has curative powers.

Exercise them as needed.

This is not the time to worry about your thighs. Or your butt. Or what your mom will think of you because you've got two bags of those miniature candy bars hidden in your kitchen cupboard. This time is about survival. If chocolate, or anything else within reason, makes you feel the tiniest bit more sane, happy, or comforted, go for it. You've got the rest of your life to obsess about carbs and sugar and transwhatevers—make yourself feel good now. Worry about being a size (fill in the blank here) later.

5

{ Have the best intentions. }

6

{ There's nothing good to see at the movies right now anyway. }

7

There is no wrong way to do this.

Okay, there probably is a wrong way,
but chances are you're not doing it.

8

❊⟩ See the humor. ⟨❊

When the poop is flying, literally, the one thing you can count on to save you is laughter. There will be moments you share with your partner and this baby that only the three of you will know. There will be dark days and the only hope of light will be having the ability to laugh, often at yourself and sometimes at one another. Know that you're not above it. That grace is on the other side of the laughter and the sheer act of doing it together is going to unite you in more ways than any darkness can divide.

9

Wearing slippers to the market is okay.

10

⋙⟨ Your body is not the same. ⟩⋙

In fact, unless major exercise or surgery is undertaken, it will probably never be the same. Have compassion, accept, and move on.

You can't blame your belly button for just sitting there, mouth gaping, wondering what the heck just happened to it, not to mention its friends, your stomach muscles. Take a look at your late-pregnancy pictures—you should be thanking your lucky stars you don't have to gather up your stomach in both arms to keep it from dragging on the ground. One day you will get that bikini back on (if you can find it). For now, give that pooch of yours a pat and be grateful it is what it is.

11

{ You will find yourself talking ad nauseam with other new parents—perhaps people with whom, pre-baby, you would have had nothing in common. Embrace these people. They may be the only ones actually interested in discussing your baby's poops—mostly because they want to know if they're the same color as their babies' poops. }

12

Order in dinner tonight.
Must include one vegetable.

13

The couch is your friend.

Consider the couch your nest. Stock appropriately: Boppy, blankies, a best friend or two. Plan on camping out for a good long while. Make yourself as comfortable as possible with fingertip access to cable, Internet, and phone. One footnote: A slipcover may be a wise investment.

14

Shopping at Target can be very therapeutic and you can't cause too much damage; go alone and take as long as you want. And as much as he loves and needs you already, there's a good chance the baby won't even notice you're gone. In fact, he'll probably take this opportunity to sleep his longest stretch of the day and be wide awake and ready when you return.

15

Take a warm, really long bath. Read trashy magazines you don't care about getting wet.

16

Call friends/sisters/mothers for support. Pick the ones who are likely to say things like, "I totally understand," "That sounds really hard," and "You're doing great" with the appropriate *yeps* and *uh-huhs* in between.

The person you don't want to call during this time is the person who had easy labor and delivery, and who now has the Gerber baby. She just doesn't know what all the fuss is about. Why, she and her husband took their little pup out to a four-course meal at nine o'clock last night and he was just a gem. Pick wisely. Stay away from the Stepford folks for a bit.

17

Breathe. Repeat.

18

This new-mother status of yours is a get-out-of-jail-free card, good for canceling family dinners, long-scheduled social engagements, or plans with people who are just too high-maintenance to be maintained right now.

19

⋇{ Wear sunglasses. }⋇

This way, if you've escaped for a few
moments of air, you're incognito. No need to
ham it up with the *barrista*, or the bookstore
clerk, or, heaven forbid, an old boyfriend.
Also, this way you can escape the applying
makeup part of going out, which, if you
attempt at this point, may prevent you
from actually getting out.

20

{ **Do one active thing today.** }

Stretching in front of *The Oprah Winfrey Show* counts.

21

{ Fall in love with your partner falling in love with your baby. }

22

{ You will be cool again. }

23

Friends who come over and offer to watch the baby for twenty minutes while you take a shower are to be commended and immediately handed said baby.

When a trusted friend or family member (who loves you and is a competent, sane individual) says, "Let me hold him for a couple minutes so you can relax," let them. You've got the rest of your life to look at this baby. Spread the newborn joy around a little.

24

Study her absolutely perfect feet until you know them by heart.

25

Do not attempt to try on your old clothes right now. This can only lead to pain of the highest order.

26

 Don't worry that you're missing out on the latest hip-and-happening restaurant. You have the rest of your life to eat in overpriced, fancy-pants establishments. Besides, no plate of pasta is worth twenty-six bucks anyway.

27

{ You cannot be all
things to all people. }

Be selfish right now. Do it for your partner.
Do it for your baby. Turn off the phone.
Shut the blinds. Put a note on the door.
Put your loving arms around this little
family of yours and hunker down. Practice
being all things to them and only them for
a little while.

28

When people come over to see the baby, you don't need to entertain them. Remember that they're not there to see you anyway.

29

※{ Become friends with your washing machine. But not your iron. }※

30

※{ Eat yogurt. }※

31

Tucks are to be trusted.

When faced with the recovery of your privates, resort to whatever means necessary. Hopefully, you will find many options for relief. But, if you find yourself wandering the drugstore aisles at ten o'clock on a Tuesday night, wondering what on earth will make this better, rest assured that Tucks will bring cold comfort to the area that has done the most for you lately.

32

There's a reason they give you a prescription for pain pills when you leave the hospital: you might need them. And, if you do, take them. After all, you don't get extra points for endurance. Get as comfortable as you can. You've got plenty of other things to be heroic about at the moment.

33

❊⟩ Use the football hold for colicky babies. It has magical powers. ⟨❊

34

{ Your baby will be this tiny for about five minutes. }

Spend a morning photographing your baby. When the house is quiet, the light is pretty, and your baby is calm, lay him on a blanket and take an entire roll of film. Take really close-up shots of his hands, feet, ears, and adorable little face. Believe it or not, one day you will not remember how small they were.

35

Put the baby on the middle of your chest,

his little feet resting on your stomach.

Breathe together.

36

❧ Hold your partner's hand. ❧

You have now met, dated, committed to, and had a child with someone. You've taken the relationship to the most serious level. There's something so sweet about taking it back to its most basic. Discover it.

37

 Mother yourself, too. }

38

Drink more water. }

39

Thankfully, it's not often you get to experience the middle of the night.

Listen closely.

40

Pay attention.

It's the little things you miss in the huge shadow of the big thing that's happening. When the baby is screaming and you are at your wit's end, notice how gently your partner is rocking her to and fro. Take a mental snapshot of the vast kindness of this person you've chosen. And who's chosen you.

41

You are in training. No one expects you to be perfect.

There will be no one voting at home on your performance. You are not going to get kicked off the island. You're coming back next week. And the next. Every day, you are learning more and more about this little person of yours. Some days will be hard. Other days will be pretty great. One minute you will have mastered feeding the baby and working the remote simultaneously, and the next you will find yourself slumped over the Diaper Champ in defeat. You will make mistakes. You will have successes. This is excellent preparation for parenthood.

42

} Hold fingers with your baby. **{**

43

} Ask your mother-in-law to come over. **{**

(If she's good with babies. And with you.)

44

⁂⧘ Sit down more. ⧙⁂

You are going on adrenaline. One day soon
that adrenaline is going to run out and
you will hit the wall. This is normal. This
is why sitting down is good, is right. In
fact, if you're reading this standing up
right now, cop a squat immediately.
Make that gently, and immediately.

45

Have someone bring you your favorite happy food (corned beef on rye, sugar snap peas, a root beer float). Eat slowly and in the company of someone who makes you laugh.

46

Don't worry if you don't get to the laundry (vacuuming, dishes, thank-you notes) today. It'll all still be there tomorrow. If, instead, you feel like lying on your big bed watching your baby sleep with both fists tucked under his chin and his cute little diapered butt up in the air, do it.

47

Whatever his schedule is today will not be his schedule tomorrow. Resist the urge to seek consistency.

"Well, yesterday he got up at four and ate every two hours, and then slept from 9:15 to 10:20, but today he got up at two and slept two hours and then didn't eat, but he did poop . . ." And on and on. It's enough to drive anyone crazy. Think of it like this: Your baby has no idea what time it is. He also has no idea that you care what time it is or he'd probably do a better job of eating, pooping, and sleeping on some sort of schedule. But one day, all on his own, he will find one. In the meanwhile, accept that there is no time in your world right now. You're on newborn time. It's just sleep, poop, eat, repeat. And that goes for you, too.

48

 Yes, he is the absolute
cutest baby ever.

49

You're right, colic sucks.

Learn how to swaddle the right way. Then learn how to swaddle, shush, and sway at the same time. Make sure your partner becomes equally skilled. Find volunteer baby-walkers. Put the baby in a sling/ BabyBjörn/stroller, and walk—around the house if you must, but in the fresh air is better. Use your baby swing. Use music. Use the vibrating seat. Use your therapist, if necessary.

50

{ Beam. Cry. Laugh. Be real. }

51

✳{ **Ask for favors.** }✳

52

 Read everything you can get your hands on, but trust your gut.

53

※{ Rally your "mom friends" for wisdom and advice. }※

54

※{ Ask for a rain check when you need one. }※

55

Just because you don't care that your shoes don't match or that your shirt is on inside out doesn't mean you are no longer a fashionista.

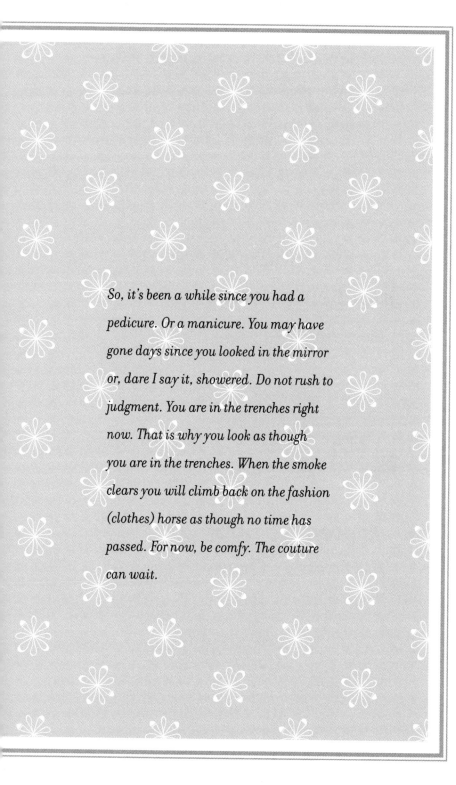

So, it's been a while since you had a pedicure. Or a manicure. You may have gone days since you looked in the mirror or, dare I say it, showered. Do not rush to judgment. You are in the trenches right now. That is why you look as though you are in the trenches. When the smoke clears you will climb back on the fashion (clothes) horse as though no time has passed. For now, be comfy. The couture can wait.

56

{ Forgive yourself for
not being perfect. }

57

{ Appreciate your
partner's efforts. }

58

Accept that during maternity leave you are not going to learn how to play golf, reorganize your closet, or get your holiday shopping done.

This is not the time to be productive. You've already produced (and reproduced) enough for the time being. Ease up on your expectation list. Throw out the to-do's and start thinking minute to minute. Spend any free moments cataloguing the wonderfulness of this little person you and your partner just made.

59

*{ Use every convenience
known to woman. }*

60

{ Close your eyes for
ten minutes. }

61

There are lots of baby things that are overrated. The baby swing is not one of them.

62

{ Yes, you still look cute. }

63

※{ Call your best friend. }※

64

Your brain, as you formerly knew it, is on temporary leave. It will return. For now, punt and be patient.

Lack of sleep, raging hormones, and serious stress can make for a slow wit. Use this time to rely on your other abilities. Like your excellent hearing. Your tolerance for weird smells. Your knowledge of where the take-out menus are. These are the skills that are really going to come in handy right now anyway. The fact that at this very moment you can't add 392 and 49 to save your life is irrelevant. It will come back. Eventually. Unless, of course, you never could add 392 and 49.

65

Go out to dinner without the baby.

Do not worry if you talk about
the baby the entire time.

66

Discover heretofore unknown talents: your dishwasher's double life as a sterilizer. Your vacuum cleaner's ability to pinch-hit as a white-noise machine. And your capacity to hold a conversation, open a "collapsible" stroller, and burp a baby at the same time.

67

※{ Call in the grandmas. }※

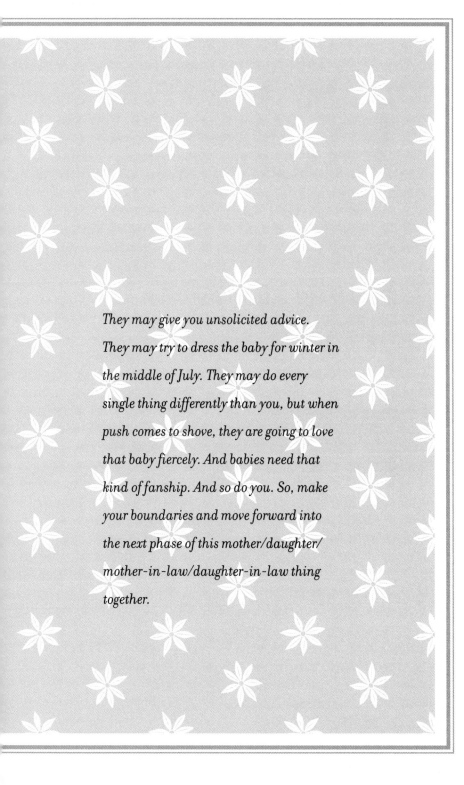

They may give you unsolicited advice. They may try to dress the baby for winter in the middle of July. They may do every single thing differently than you, but when push comes to shove, they are going to love that baby fiercely. And babies need that kind of fanship. And so do you. So, make your boundaries and move forward into the next phase of this mother/daughter/ mother-in-law/daughter-in-law thing together.

68

 **Walk.**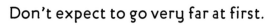

Don't expect to go very far at first.

It's not the distance, it's the motion.

69

If you are bottle-feeding, premeasure your powdered formula and put it in one of those three-way plastic separator gadgets. This way, you have exactly the right amount to dump into the bottle when your baby suddenly decides she's hungry, RIGHT THIS VERY MINUTE.

70

Always bring an extra
change of clothes.

(For both of you.)

71

Have a picnic, just the three of you. On the living room carpet, if necessary.

72

❧{ Do not make any big plans. }❧

This includes any new, drastically
different hairstyles.

73

 For good and for bad, your life will not stay this way.

74

❦ Love your partner. ❦

Demonstrate this more than you think is necessary.

75

One day you will get a Mother's Day card commemorating all of this.

76

{ Let him sleep. }

Don't think that if you wake
him, he will sleep longer tonight.
He won't. He'll just be cranky
today *and* tonight.

77

If you are breast-feeding, take a few minutes to congratulate yourself on the achievement. After nine months of managing to keep an actual person alive inside your body, you're now generously extending the invitation indefinitely.

78

*❧ He loves your singing.

Yes, *your* singing.* ❧

This is the part of motherhood that can do what years of therapy may have been unable to: give your self-esteem a huge boost. To this baby, you are the moon and the stars and the sun and everything in between. You are perfection. You are without compare; he doesn't know how your mom would do it, or how the really "good" mother who lives down the street would do it. He only knows, and cares, about you. About being around you and with you. Accept that, during this one time in your life, expectations have already been met. The moment he opens his eyes and gazes into yours, bingo, you start with 100 percent of his adoration. So, for as much as you were prepared to love this baby with all of your heart, being loved by all his may be the first of many surprises that lie ahead.

79

 Managing an infant is a whole lot different than managing a department. Accept this.

80

Have breakfast— even if it's 1:00 p.m.

There's something that feels sane about breakfast. Eggs, bacon, pancakes— preferably made by someone else—are comforting. There's the illusion, at least, that all is well. After all, we are eating. We are functioning. Break out the maple syrup—and don't dare count a single calorie. For the time being, fat does not exist. Sugar is merely an ingredient. If the smell of your mom's biscuits makes your house feel more like the home it's becoming, inhale and inhale deeply. And then, by all means, eat.

81

Join a new-mom's group.

Find out there are at least twenty other moms who are as delirious, scared, and elated as you are.

82

83

{ Do not buy too many
newborn diapers. }

You'll be amazed at how

fast she'll grow.

84

 Don't buy too many newborn toys.

She will be more interested in eating, sleeping, or you.

85

It may seem like you are the only one whose world has ever become this chaotic, this sleepless, this teeny-bit psychotic, but you aren't.

No one wants to admit that the newborn time, for lots of people, is tough. Just because everybody else at the new-mom's group has makeup on and their hair done doesn't mean they're doing better than you. Maybe they had to apply makeup because they spent the morning crying right along with their baby. Maybe their hair is done because they never went to sleep last night. Regardless, admitting the challenge of this time is not saying you're not a good mom, or that you are not desperately in love with this infant. What it is saying is that getting three-and-a-half minutes of sleep a night is not normal. That not knowing how to comfort, or feed, or hold this brand-new, tiny little ball of a person can be frightening. You are going to get the hang of it. It might not be today, but one day soon, you will. For now, know that even though it sometimes seems like you're alone, you're not.

86

❧ You will never have been so happy to hear someone pass gas. ❧

87

Do not be alarmed that
entire conversations
revolve around poop—
the consistency, the
frequency, and the color.

88

Many new moms agree that one month in newborn time equals about three months in regular time. Which means each day can feel about three days long. "Was it today that we walked to the park? Wow. That seems like days ago." There's a reason time is moving slowly: there's lots of growing going on, on your part and on your baby's. Growth takes time. Maybe it's nature's way of giving both of you an opportunity to do all the getting-to-know-you that you both need, without being rushed.

89

{ Go to your six-week checkup. Be honest about how you're feeling. }

If you've been crying for three weeks straight and have a hard time making it out of bed each day, say so. If you're having pain, or something doesn't feel quite right, speak up. If you're doing just great, thank you very much, share that, too. Your doctor is there to see you: be seen. You deserve nothing less.

90

 Buy yourself a book on tape. Better yet, order it online.

91

❋{ Kiss. }❋

92

{ Multitask:

Nap with your baby. }

93

You are still you.

Just you with leaky, DD breasts,
wrinkled shirts, and empty take-
out containers littering your
kitchen counter.

94

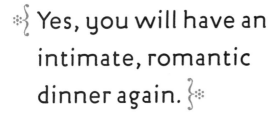

Yes, you will have an intimate, romantic dinner again.

(Without a small, grumpy guest in attendance.)

95

Use e-mail to connect with your friends and family instead of the phone. This way you don't have to spend every few seconds saying, "Wait a minute, I think the baby is crying."

96

❧ Meet your neighbors. ❧

We live in a world where two-car garages are taking the place of front doors. We pull into the driveway, click the remote, drive in, click again, and disappear inside of our McMansions, never knowing our potential new best friend down the street. The one who not only has the most amazing recipe for Chicken Provençal, but will actually make it for you and bring it over to your starving and grateful little family on your third night home from the hospital. Take this opportunity to walk out your front door and knock on someone else's. You have the perfect calling card: no one can close the door on a precious, adorable little baby. Or the harried new mom he hangs out with.

97

{ Make peace with the fact that someone who doesn't even have control of his arms and legs, let alone his bodily functions, determines the success of your day. }

98

Exchange three-minute shoulder rubs with your partner.

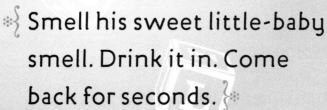

99

❖{ Smell his sweet little-baby smell. Drink it in. Come back for seconds. }❖

100

Write everything down.

Not just feeding and pooping times,
but phone messages, gifts (with
descriptions, not just "toy"), and
random thoughts about your baby.
You will treasure them once you
regain sleep and consciousness.

101

Two words:

explosive poop.

Be prepared, not alarmed.

102

{ Sanity is a relative term. }

103

A woman has lost her way in a foreign city. Looking for guidance, she walks into an establishment and announces, "I'm lost." The owner answers, "No, you're not. You are right here." Be right here, now.

104

❧ Your mother would be proud. ❧

*It's amazing how much becoming a mother
makes you think about your own. Whether
she's long gone or right next to you at this
moment changing Junior's diaper, know
that your effort to get to this moment, your
effort to care about what kind of mother
you are, shows that, no matter what your
relationship, your mother must have done
something right. Even if it was just
bringing you into the world. And now that
you've brought someone into the world,
you know this is no easy thing.*

105

 You are getting

better at this.

106

{ One day, her personality is going to knock you off your feet. }

There will come a time when she will look at you and say, "You are my sweet mommy, and I want to be with you forever." She will look at a single bump of paint on the wall and ask where the bump's mommy, daddy, and brother are. One day this little person with no neck strength and bad gas will charm you with her panache. Until then, imagine.

107

Have a spare, clean cover
for your changing pad.

108

ꙮ{ Practice infant massage. }ꙮ

Even if you have no training.

Just do what you think

would feel good to you.

109

Love her.

Love her.

Love her.

There are things you will fail at as a mother. Times when you don't have the right answer. Days when you don't want to read another story, play another game, or explain one more thing. There are all sorts of ways you will come up short and will disappoint you both. But if you love her truly, madly, deeply, with all of your heart, and you show it, then the most important part of the job has been done.

110

 Be gentle.

Especially on yourself.

111

 You may feel neurotic.
You may be neurotic.
This is to be expected,
even celebrated
among friends.

112

❈⟩ Hold your tongue. ⟨❈

*You may say things in the heat of the
moment that you will regret. You may
explode at the very people who love you
and this baby most. The best thing you
can do when you have just the thing you
want to say at just the moment you are
dying to say it, is wait. Restrain yourself
for another five minutes. Or an hour. Or a
day. Wait until you're feeling a little more
sane. There will always be another time
to lay it all out there, after you've had a
chance to think about what exactly "it all"
is. And whether laying it out there will
help anybody, or just hurt everybody.*

113

 You still call your mom to ask how long chicken lasts after it's defrosted. Think of all the other stuff she may know.

Ask.

114

{ Be humble. }

115

{ The new-mommy friend who is always perfect, clean, and groomed, and who has a perfect, clean, and groomed baby, is to be avoided. Or at least held under suspicion until you learn her secrets. }

116

Be stingy with your time. But be generous with your goodwill.

The days of two-hour phone sessions with your best friend are probably over. Lingering over coffee while your terminally single friend laments the state of men is most likely a distant memory. Lazy mornings in bed with your sweetheart? Not for now. Yes, you will have more free time again, but it may never be what it was pre-baby. It'll come in fits and starts. So, for now, snag a ten-minute heart-to-heart with your dearest friend while you're feeding the baby. Send your partner a quick love-text at work. Write a personal ad for your single friend at 2:00 a.m. when, for some reason, the baby has actually fallen asleep but now you can't. There is still room for all the love to be expressed. You just need to find creative—and quicker—avenues to express it.

117

Sleep at 4:00 p.m. on a Tuesday and feel completely within your rights.

It's probably been a few years since you passed out on the couch in the middle of the afternoon. The last time it happened, you probably had a hangover remedy in one hand and the remote in the other. Now, it's a burp rag and a binky. Regardless, this is the time to take full advantage of dozing off whenever the opportunity strikes. The moment your elaborate routine of sleep-inducing tactics works on your little insomniac, lay down immediately and close your eyes, wherever, whenever. When he sleeps, you sleep. And if you can't sleep, at least reacquaint yourself with the insides of your eyelids for a few minutes.

118

If you have washed at least one body part today, consider yourself clean.

119

❧ Don't wish this time away.
You will get that wish soon
enough. ❧

120

❧ Yes, this much spit-up
is normal. ❧

(Generally.)

121

❧ Have faith in your
own judgment.
And in your partner's. ❧

122

⁂{ You are not the only one
who can take care of him.
And if you are, ask for help. }⁂

123

❧ Do not hold back one little bit of your heart for fear of it getting broken. It's too late for that anyway. ❧

124

A pacifier can be a good thing. True, it might be hard to break her of it one day, but that's then. By that time, you should be sleeping more—which means anything will be more manageable.

125

When you think you just can't do it
another minute, remember how very, very
much you and your partner prayed for,
hoped for, or luckily stumbled into this
pregnancy. How grateful and overcome
you were the day your baby arrived. And
then take a deep breath, give him a
squeeze, and keep on keeping on.

126

Staring at your newborn is fun

for a few minutes or hours. After that, you're going to need something else to do. Get yourselves out of the house at least once a day after the first couple of weeks and find it.

127

The witching hour exists. If your baby doesn't have one, consider yourself lucky and keep it to yourself.

The baby who sleeps well now might be the very one who doesn't sleep his entire second year of life. The one who takes a bottle easily today may be the one who won't eat a single vegetable as a toddler. If you happen to luck into a sweet, easy newborn, count your blessings and know, on this one, at this time, you're skating. Good for you. And when your four-year-old won't give up the pacifier or your two-year-old keeps taking his pants off in public, know that this, too, is all par for the course.

128

Resist the temptation to criticize other mothers or mothering techniques. No one has a degree in this field to date.

129

You have way too many clothes for him.

There is no way he can wear them all
before he outgrows them. This is fine.
Start the hand-me-down box now,
or better yet, donate them to a crisis
nursery or children's home, where
they will surely get some use.

130

{ Getting no sleep is a good
excuse for almost anything. }

You no longer have to feel

guilty about parking tickets,

bad-hair days, or cutting people

off in traffic.

131

There is no way to look good, or even somewhat dignified, pumping breast milk. Don't fight this.

132

You are a better mother than you think you are.

133

{ You might not need a wipe warmer. But you definitely need wipes. Lots. }

Keep them in the car, your purse, your diaper bag, the back bedroom, and anywhere else your little one might decide to decorate with a bodily fluid of one kind or another.

134

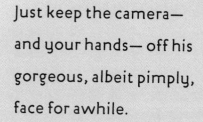

{ Baby acne clears up on its own. }

Just keep the camera—
and your hands— off his
gorgeous, albeit pimply,
face for awhile.

135

{ This may not even be his actual hair. This is baby hair. Do not panic if it is alarming in color, texture, or amount. }

Your baby is not going to look like this forever. Even if you think he's the most adorable thing ever, he probably isn't, at least right now. But he will be. He's going to get chubbier and smilier and more delicious every day. Being able to hold his head up on his own will do a lot for his charisma. Prepare to be drunk on his adorableness soon.

136

{ Whatever works for your
family, works. }

137

There is something that will make her stop crying. You may not know what it is right now, but it's out there, waiting for you to discover it.

It seems like every baby has a different little combination lock on her crying. Finding that perfect bounce—or shush, or dance, or walk, or carrier, or swing—that will comfort her will be your mission in life for the next few months, and one day you will find it and you will cling to it as though it were a life raft and your house were the Titanic. And then, all of a sudden, one afternoon, it may not work, because she changed the combination on you, and you will panic. But don't. Because now you will know her better. It will take you half the time to find the key than it took you the first time. Now you will have two ways to comfort her when it's three o'clock in the morning and you both need comfort and peace so very much. This is the beginning of becoming an expert on your baby. Congratulations.

138

There is a reason sleep deprivation is used as a torture device. It is torture. There is nothing fun about it. You will never wake up from a night of absolutely no sleep and say, "You know what? I think I'm getting used to this."

139

This little wonder of yours is going to be expensive. Everything about him is going to cost just a bit more, or maybe a lot more, than you expected. Don't overwhelm yourself trying to figure out how you're going to pay for college if just *diapers* are this expensive. Worry about paying for diapers now; worry about paying for college later.

140

❧ Consult the professionals. ❧

Doulas, nannies, lactation consultants, pediatricians, obstetricians, advice nurses, labor and delivery nurses: they know things. It's actually their job to know things. Be a good student. Take notes and listen. But don't be afraid to question, either.

141

⸙{ This is not necessarily your child's personality. }⸙

Don't let the "he's-been-like-this-since-the-day-he-was-born" stories scare you. After all, there aren't many colicky, narcoleptic adults running around throwing up on everyone and crying. He will become himself. Who that is remains to be seen.

142

Don't let the currently blank "baby book" intimidate you. Make notes on scraps of paper for now if that's all you can handle. Just write. You will both appreciate it someday.

143

Diapers, meals complete with salad and dessert, and quick visits where you get to lie down for a couple minutes sans baby are the kind of gifts you need right now. Let people know. A flowering plant may not do a whole lot for you at this moment in your life.

144

 Don't compare your baby.
Don't compare yourself.
You are both doing just fine.

145

Get everything ready for the bath before the baby gets anywhere near the water. Use a towel with a hood. Use a mild baby soap that doubles as shampoo. Remember to wait for a real bath until the umbilical cord falls off.

146

 Don't worry about what fancy stroller you should get. You can get your real wheels later.

Instead, use one of those inexpensive aluminum frame ones where the infant car seat snaps right on. This way, the baby can stay in the same seat from car to stroller and back again without waking up. Plus, it weighs a lot less than a real stroller. Important when you're getting used to carrying twenty pounds of baby gear around with you.

147

Take a drive.
Alone.
Windows open.

148

{ Ask a girlfriend to go to a movie. A chick one. Bring tissues. And Junior Mints. }

149

{ **Cloth diapers are wonderful.** }
Sometimes for the tush,
but they also make ideal
burp rags. When trying
to stem a tide of spit-up,
thickness and absorbency
become quite important.

150

You are someone's mother.

Someone's world.

Someone's everything.

Isn't that something?

⁂{ acknowledgments }⁂

This book about motherhood wouldn't have been brought to
life without a whole lot of mothering. Much gratitude to:

~ My agent, the amazing Andrea Barzvi at ICM, and the
talented Marnie Cochran, my editor at Random House.

~ My own mom, Stephanie Beeman. Thank you for doing
a wonderful job on #109.

~ The moms in my life who inspire me daily with their
patience, their humor, and most of all, their friendship.
You know who you are.

~ To Dick Broder, for believing. For setting the bar so high.
For not letting me change my major to psychology.

~ And to Reese and Finn, for choosing me to come through.
And to Chris, for everything.

❧ about the author ❧

An advertising copywriter for more than a decade,
GERALYN BRODER MURRAY lives with her husband
and two young children in Sacramento, California.

www.geralynbrodermurray.blogspot.com